Poetry 'n Praise

Creative Devotions

LENORE C. UDDYBACK-FORTSON

Library of Congress Control Number:		2012921661
ISBN:	Hardcover	978-1-4797-5214-0
	Softcover	978-1-4797-5213-3
	eBook	978-1-4797-5215-7

Scripture taken from the King James Version of the Bible.

This book was printed in the United States of America.

Rev. date: 05/23/2014

To order additional copies of this book, contact:
Xlibris LLC
1-888-795-4274
www.Xlibris.com
Orders@Xlibris.com
538208

Contents

Dedication

This book is dedicated to my best friend and loving husband, Wesley L. Fortson, who always holds it down for his family; and Noah Christian Fortson, my beautiful blessing, who held me accountable and cheered me "over the finish line" with this project. It is my humble offering to My Heavenly Father who designed me, knew me when I was still in my mother's womb, breathed purpose into my life, and most importantly, gave His only begotten son that I might have eternal life. For Him, and Him alone, I live.

I pray my words penetrate hearts, lead lost souls to Christ and undergird and uplift those in need of encouragement. To God Be The Glory!

Praise ye the Lord. Praise God in his sanctuary: praise him in the firmament of his power. Praise him for his mighty acts: praise him according to his excellent greatness. Praise him with the sound of the trumpet: praise him with the psaltery and harp. Praise him with the timbrel and dance: praise him with stringed instruments and organs. Praise him upon the loud cymbals: praise him upon the high sounding cymbals. Let everything that hath breath praise the Lord. Praise ye the Lord.

Psalm 150 (King James Version)

Poetry 'n Praise

My voice,
longing to be heard
beckons the words
to articulate
an inaudible cry,
utterances buried deep within me
long before this moment.

A well of gratitude
reflecting years of
undeserved grace
and
misunderstood mercies
bursts
releasing
extemporaneous energy.

Erupting emotions
ignite all senses
sending
Hallelujahs
flowing freely;
spontaneous worship
elevating my spirit to more profound praise.

The Lord is my light and my salvation; whom shall I fear? the Lord is the strength of my life; of whom shall I be afraid?

Psalm 27:1 (KJV)

I Can

I can do all things through Christ who strengthens me
my head held high
my eyes focused upward
walking tall
moving forward
led by faith
with the grace of the Holy Spirit holding me steady.

I can do all things through Christ who strengthens me
without hesitation
in spite of any obstacle
in the face of persecution
My God is always faithful.

I can do all things through Christ who strengthens me
soaring above my aspirations
leaving behind my inhibitions
leaping over my limitations
tightly gripping my Savior's hand.

I can do all things through Christ who strengthens me
living
loving
laughing
shouting praises to his name.

Yes, oh yes!
I CAN do all things through Christ who strengthens me
Because of that,
my life will never be
the same.

Blessed is the man that walketh not in the counsel of the ungodly, nor standeth in the way of sinners, nor sitteth in the seat of the scornful. But his delight is in the law of the Lord; and in his law doth he meditate day and night.

Psalm 1:1-2 (KJV)

For Christ I Live

His image
emblazes my heart
for all to see,
and know without question
whom I serve—to whom I belong

I have taken up His Cross
standing firm with all I have
ready to serve
awed by

The ultimate sacrifice made
when He poured out His blood at Calvary
to redeem,
embrace
lost, hurting souls like me
through a priceless act of love,
a selfless offering given
to those willing to accept its eternal gift.

Humbly,
I fall to my knees in receipt;
eyes opened to new mercies
through the wonder of my salvation.

He that dwelleth in the secret place of the most High shall abide under the shadow of the Almighty. I will say of the Lord, He is my refuge and my fortress; my God; in him will I trust

Psalm 91:1-2 (KJV)

Deep Well of Wisdom

With outstretched hands
A wide-open heart and
a quiet, willing spirit
I kneel
Anticipating the presence
Of my Heavenly Father

Humbly on my knees
I again come
to taste and to see
That the Lord is good

I remain
Longing for even a drop of the dew
That clings to His deep well of wisdom
A word
Released in a whisper
Echoing volumes
Offering a jarring splash of life's true meaning
Reaffirming my purpose
Refreshing my dusty core
Leaving me wanting
Yearning
Crying out for His full embrace of Glory.

And yet,
In a moment,
Time suspends
And I am filled.

I rise
Full
My mind renewed
And once more
I am ready to face the world.

I will bless the Lord at all times: his praise shall continually be in my mouth. My soul shall make her boast in the Lord: the humble shall hear thereof, and be glad. O magnify the Lord with me, and let us exalt his name together.

Psalm 34:1-3 (KJV)

Another Level

I am moving to a deeper level
of devotion,
spiritual readiness
for Kingdom action.
A call
so distinct
so strong
leading to a destination unknown.

No excuses!
No reason to hesitate before
stepping onto my path
stretched out before me by my Redeemer.
No room for anything but
obedience without pause.

Steps directed by faith,
purpose
leaving behind traces of my light
for longing souls—distressed and empty
reflecting
He that is within me

I take each step
with my sword and my shield,
excited
about "around-the-corner" evidence of His love
that never ceases to amaze.
Personal strokes of color
that brighten my horizon
and make clear
what life is meant to be,
the life He has for me
if I trust,
believe,
seek,
I will find Him,
and can follow Him
to a higher level.

Hear my prayer, O Lord, and let my cry come unto thee. Hide not thy face from me in the day when I am in trouble; incline thine ear unto me: in the day when I call answer me speedily.

Psalm 102:1-2 (KJV)

Tears

tears tell my story
of prayers silenced
when selfish rebellion
seized my thoughts

needs aching for utterance
grew faint
remained hidden
betrayed by a shame-stained heart
in avoidance of confession

eyes blinded by a carnal perspective
spied a wearisome me
devoid of focus
pierced by the hollowness of my commitment
shaken by the echo of false promises
rendered weak by a reckless refusal to repent
and return to the foot of the Cross
where peace is promised
from everlasting to everlasting, leaving me with

tears that stung with regret
time lost
swept away by each enemy lie embraced
opportunity evaporated
destiny disturbed—seemingly without cause
revealing the startling reflection of brokenness
until the Word,
the truth
punctured pride releasing

tears that flow freely now
celebrating a relationship restored
renewal, revival
precious moments redeemed by grace
splashes of refreshing
humble repositioning
in receipt of blessings
always intended for me.

Blessed is he whose transgression is forgiven, whose sin is covered. Blessed is the man unto whom the Lord imputeth not iniquity, and in whose spirit there is no guile. When I kept silence, my bones waxed old through my roaring all the day long. For day and night thy hand was heavy upon me: my moisture is turned into the drought of summer. Selah. I acknowledged my sin unto thee, and mine iniquity have I not hid. I said, I will confess my transgressions unto the Lord; and thou forgavest the iniquity of my sin. Selah.

Psalm 32:1-5 (KJV)

Next Chapter

I awakened this morning
To a new chapter of life, of love
When the radiance of Your perfect light
Stroked my brow
Electrifying everything within me

And I was lifted
from the sustained slumber of sadness that
I long allowed to steal my joy

I now accept with praise
The gifts you have given
And present them as my simple offering to You

Stepping into the sunlight of my destiny—my Hallelujah Horizon
I plant my feet firmly
In the peace of Your promises
My spirit shielded
By Your love and grace

I yield my will to Yours this day
Moment by moment by moment
No longer succumbing
To the strength of my yesterdays
Or cowering
Hiding from the powerful unknown
Of my tomorrows
Instead
I stand rejoicing
Ready to follow
The path of righteousness
You have stretched out before me.

I will praise thee, O Lord, with my whole heart; I will shew forth all thy marvelous works. I will be glad and rejoice in thee: I will sing praise to thy name, O thou most High.

Psalm 9:1-2(KJV)

O Lord

I long to hear Your voice
O Lord
And anticipate
The sound of life
Speaking peace beyond measure
Directly to the core of my heart
Breathing new hope into
My strained and long-suffering spirit

I long to see Your face
O Lord
To hide myself
Without shame
In the embrace
Of Your glory and grace
Humbly basking in
A single moment of worship

I long to feel Your presence
O Lord
So that I
If but only for one second
Can know
Without question
The wonder of pure joy

It is You I seek to mirror
O Lord
Your heart
I want to know and share
Your purpose for me
I desire to fulfill
Your will
I pray,
Be done.
Amen

The heavens declare the glory of God; and the firmament sheweth his handiwork.

Psalm 19:1 (KJV)

A Single Moment of Praise

For a moment, my world slowed
long enough for me
to really watch God at work.
A snow fall that embraced its landing
blanketed all within reach
in winter perfection.

It was a day not yet marked by the stain
of a busy life zooming without pause
allowing time
to take in,
marvel at
such utter beauty.

It all slowed to a peaceful pace
that provided perspective,
and allowed sheer gratitude to surface,
inviting praise,
worship,
joy;
and in a moment,
a single moment
the little things triumphed!

Praise ye the Lord. Sing unto the Lord a new song, and his praise in the congregation of saints.

Psalm 149:1 (KJV)

God's Family

We are God's family
the living pulse of His love
melded faces, molded to reflect His very image
hands that offer the touch of His comfort
hearts tightly embraced beyond bloodlines
ears attuned to the screaming silence of peace
that steadies us beyond all understanding
assuring strength arises from a place found deep in the spirit
and slowly reveals the riches that come
as we give of ourselves a portion—
each precious gift bestowed by our Father
and wait with Heavenly hope
anticipating
the arrival
the return
of those lost and in need
of the One Who Finds.

Give ear to my words, O Lord, consider my meditation. Hearken unto the voice of my cry, my King, and my God: for unto thee will I pray. My voice shalt thou hear in the morning, O Lord; in the morning will I direct my prayer unto thee, and will look up.

Psalm 5:1-3 (KJV)

Morning

In the silence of the morning
I catch my mind racing
To imagined adventures
In my future

Leaping over hurdles that spring
Like wildfire
Embracing the unchanging hand of my Savior

In the wake of the sun's first appearance
I dance through "mind's-eye" images
Mazes of foggy memories
That often appear
Reminding me of where I've been
Encouraging me to continue moving
Toward the dreams
Whose promises keep me company.

The Lord is my rock, and my fortress, and my deliverer; my God, my strength, in whom I will trust; my buckler, and the horn of my salvation, and my high tower.

Psalm 18:2 (KJV)

Seren

The vision of promise,
A life promised,
A life given.
The promise of an anointed life anticipated
With thanksgiving.

Eye-opening wonder at the awe of miracles
Done by the hands of a Master,
Lord,
Redeemer,
Deliverer,
Loving Father,
Faithful Friend,
Perfect Creator.

Lord, I cry unto thee: make haste unto me; give ear unto my voice, when I cry unto thee. Let my prayer be set forth before thee as incense; and the lifting up of my hands as the evening sacrifice. Set a watch, O Lord, before my mouth; keep the door of my lips. Incline not my heart to any evil thing, to practice wicked works with men that work iniquity: and let me not eat of their dainties.

Psalm 141:1-4 (KJV)

My Prayer

deliver me from my feelings,
oh Lord—
of offence,
annoyance,
rejection,
so that i might target Your truth
for my focus;

and deliver me to
a constant state of forgiveness,
so that Christ radiates from my heart
and is revealed when i smile,
even through tears;

shift my thoughts
to a place that is pure,
lovely,
admirable,
excellent;

propel me above my flesh,
that i might rest in the spirit,
drawing comfort from The Cross,
covered by Your blood,
directed by Your hand;

remove me from the mire i'm stuck in;
wash me clean of my each and every sin,
preparing me for the purpose
that reigns in my destiny;

bathe me in humility,
that i might perpetually fall
to my knees in gratitude,
without prodding,
clearly bowing to
the Lord of my life;

enable me to resist
traps,
schemes,
temptations
that lurk
and plots to foil
simple successes of each new day;

let love be the badge
i wear freely,
revealing to all
my pursuit of peace;
and my ties to Your Kingdom
an anchor in this world,
bracing me through battles
blown in
by winds of discontent;

let me be
the very essence
of the woman you envisioned when you made me—
embodying all you have given me;
and embrace without question
the person of God You created me to be.

Bless the Lord, O my soul: and all that is within me, bless his holy name. Bless the Lord, O my soul, and forget not his benefits. Who forgiveth all thine iniquities; who healeth all thy diseases; Who redeemeth thy life from destruction; who crowneth thee with lovingkindness and tender mercies; who satisfieth thy mouth with good things; so that thy youth is renewed like the eagle's.

Psalm 103:1-5 (KJV)

My Lord

I love my Lord
He owns my heart
He gives me hope
And Sweet peace
When I cease to struggle
And fall freely
Into His never-ending arms
Seeking real rest

There, I am protected
Blanketed with mercies
Shielded by grace from the bitter winds of sorrow
That surge
When my eyes lose their intended view

He reminds me of who I am meant to be
And reveals another part of my purpose
With the gift of each morning

I am beholden
No longer my own
I will serve Him
Worship at His throne
With all that I am
With every breath, offer praise
And pray for redeemable time
To share my victory in Christ
To the blessing of others.

O Lord our Lord, how excellent is thy name in all the earth! who hast set thy glory above the heavens.

Psalm 8:1 (KJV)

Only You

Through You, Only You,
life is eternal
wisdom is Heaven-sent
hearts are healed
mercies are new each morning
all things are possible.

In You, and You only,
peace is constant
hope is evident
life is transformative
belief bears all burdens
pure rest restores
spirits soar
and truth reigns.

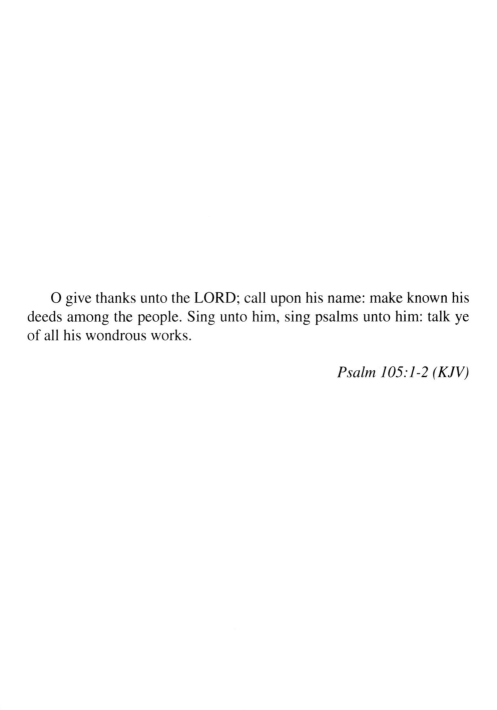

O give thanks unto the LORD; call upon his name: make known his deeds among the people. Sing unto him, sing psalms unto him: talk ye of all his wondrous works.

Psalm 105:1-2 (KJV)

When Words Fail

Yours is the very hand
by which I was given life,
life anew
Your sacrifice
Removed my stain
of sin-filled guilt, hidden shame
and breathed new hope
into what once was an uncertain future
a miserable path leading to a dead end

I am no longer empty
Joy and peace abound

A contentment I never knew
Embraces each new day
Shielding my vision from dissatisfaction
Gently refocusing me
on true blessings that appear without warning
and prompt tears—an instant release revealing my gratitude
Conveying the messages of my heart
Saying everything I want to say
Deep spirit-filled thanks
That otherwise might go unheard
When words fail.

How amiable are thy tabernacles, O LORD of hosts! My soul longeth, yea, even fainteth for the courts of the LORD: my heart and my flesh crieth out for the living God.

Psalm 84:1-2

Yours to Use

I am an instrument-Yours to use
Ready
Eager
Open

Pour into me
So that I may pour into others
The hope you so freely give
to mend tattered hearts

I remain a work in progress
Waiting
Anticipating peace
Brought through the Potter's touch
Smoothing rough areas of my life

I bask in Your vision of me
Celebrate the person I am to become
A true reflection of Your Son
Standing on the foundation
of truth, obedience, submission, sacrifice
In a never-ending effort
To Glorify Your Name.

I will sing of the mercies of the LORD forever: with my mouth will I make known thy faithfulness to all generations. For I have said, Mercy shall be built up forever: thy faithfulness shalt thou establish in the very heavens.

Psalm 89:1-2 (KJV)

God's Best Seller

The author of my life
He created my story, developed my character
Finished my plot
Writing the first word
Blowing the ink dry on the last

And tho' He will not let me see how it ends
By His grace, I can turn each page
Begin each new chapter in faith
Knowing it is sufficient
To sustain me
To and thru the climax
Allowing for rest in Him
As I journey toward the conclusion.

Truly my soul waiteth upon God: from him cometh my salvation. He only is my rock and my salvation; he is my defence; I shall not be greatly moved.

Psalm 62:1-2 (KJV)

New Eyes of Hope

Brightness blinds me
Warms me
Leads me
Holds me
Encourages me
With each step I take toward triumph

Dark, dismal days
Release ambitions
Once arrested by fear
And purpose declares victory
I am moved to tears

A deafening mantra of promises materializes
Removing all doubt
And life takes shape
In ways
Only realized in dreams
Vivid
Active
Unashamed

Perfectly orchestrated images
That appear in living color
Right before once-downcast eyes
Now lifted
In the direction
From whence cometh my help
And it comes
And I can now see it
Through new eyes of hope.

I waited patiently for the Lord; and he inclined unto me, and heard my cry. He brought me up also out of an horrible pit, out of the miry clay, and set my feet upon a rock, and established my goings. And he hath put a new song in my mouth, even praise unto our God: many shall see it, and fear, and shall trust in the Lord.

Psalm 40:1-3 (KJV)

Swept Away

When I think about how You saved me
Kept me
Nestled me
In the palm of Your hand
Strengthening me
Surrounding me with Your protection
Guiding me, leading me through the power of Your spirit
Shielding me with the breadth of your wisdom

When I ponder the very ways
Your hand has remained upon me
Covered me
Shrouded me with your love
Even when I tried to turn, walk away
Knowing better, feigned indifference
Stuck in my selfish, unyielding stance

When I stop and really look back
With open, honest, unfiltered eyes
That see without filter
Absorb the ways in which
You gifted me
Lovingly prepared me—even through hardship and trial
For the journey You planned my life to take
I am swept away
By the overwhelming current of joy Your blessings bring
And without warning
Thankful tears stream in submission.

O come, let us sing unto the Lord: let us make a joyful noise to the rock of our salvation. Let us come before his presence with thanksgiving, and make a joyful noise unto him with psalms.

Psalm 95:1-2 (KJV)

Triumphant Return

No trumpets
Drums
Or fanfare
Announced the occasion
But my heart rejoiced
And sang praises to the heavens!

I will love thee, O Lord, my strength.

Psalm 18:1 (KJV)

Morning Glory

The sun is happy
As it rises to greet us
With light that welcomes another day

Its rays stretch over
Each flower
Courting their brilliance
As they shyly give in
To a shining smile

And from the bird's home
Their good morning song
Refreshing the air
With a sweet melody
That sings praises to God
As life goes on.

As the hart panteth after the water brooks, so panteth my soul after thee, o God. My soul thirsteth for God, for the living God: when shall I come and appear before God? My tears have been my meat day and night, while they continually say unto me, Where is thy God? When I remember these things, I pour out my soul in me: for I had gone with the multitude, I went with them to the house of God, with the voice of joy and praise, with a multitude that kept holyday.

Psalm 42:1-4 (KJV)

Sweet Remembrances

The sun smiled on me this morning.
Warming my face and tickling my ear,
It whispered sweet remembrances
Of God's Glory,
God's Grace,
The many ways He has touched me
And made me whole, extending His Holy hand
Over the damaged areas
Of my soul
Those in need of repair—and there were many,
Still are many
In need of His touch,
Areas I remain too afraid to explore
Despite His assurance.

So patiently He waits
For my faith to lead me
To the place
Where my Heavenly Father
Always demonstrates his unconditional love,
Compassion,
Deep understanding of my thoughts, fears and cares.

He waits
For me to cast them onto Him
To take His yoke
With ease
And with rest
Because He cares for me.

Make a joyful noise unto the Lord, all ye lands. Serve the Lord with gladness: come before his presence with singing. Know ye that that Lord he is God: it is he that hath made us, and not we ourselves; we are his people, and the sheep of his pasture.

Psalm 100:1-3 (KJV)

Earth's Salute to Autumn

In the stillness of the morning
At the sun's first stretch
A parade of the earth's soldiers
Covered in a crown of warm hues
Stand alert
Ready
Regal
Until a gentle nudge
Beckons their attention
And they bow in succession
At the wind's command
Rejoicing
Saluting the majesty, pageantry
Of God's Glory
When autumn arrives
And presents it colors.

God is our refuge and strength, a very present help in trouble. Therefore will not we fear, though the earth be removed, and though the mountains be carried into the midst of the sea; Though the waters thereof roar and be troubled, though the mountains shake with the swelling thereof. Selah.

Psalm 46:1-3 (KJV)

Heart Peace

The precious calm
of our Heavenly Father's
sweeping power
engulfing all sadness, offering
the sweet assurance of love, security and faithful assistance
through life's most troubled seasons.

Pure understanding,
which anchors emotions
that rage with fear
desperate to determine
the next step in a predestined journey
the unanticipated awe
of never-ending mercy and grace

An embrace of the spirit
which follows a chorus of His wisdom
coming when most needed,
echoing
in a still, small voice
declared devotion.

An outstretched, unchanging hand offered
to lead a willing soul
step
by step
by step
by step.

Restore unto me the joy of thy salvation; and uphold me with thy free spirit.

Psalm 51:12 (KJV)

Restoration

Battered
I collapsed
Under life's weight
Knocked off-balance
By constant waves of inadequacy
Sent to discourage
Dismay
Destroy
Further shifting my stance
To a pit of uncertainty.

I was going under
ashamed
of who I thought I was,
claimed to be
The broken pieces reflecting lies
Failure.

Then I looked to my Mighty GOD in Heaven
Whose wonders never cease
Whose mercies are new every morning.
Who finishes every good work
Who spoke promise over me before I even entered this earth
And my limp spirit found the strength to rejoice
Crying Hallelujah
Thirsting for Living Water
Refreshed in the midst of a downpour
offering newly offered Grace.

The Lord is my shepherd; I shall not want. He maketh me to lie down in green pastures: he leadeth me beside the still waters.

Psalm 23:1-2 (KJV)

I'm All In

No more half-steppin'
I am All in!

No longer will I limp thru life
With one foot in the world.
God is calling me to run
to every corner of the earth
to proclaim the Good news
of the ultimate sacrifice
that brought the gift of eternal life
to a fallen and deprived world.

No more falling prey to the desires of my flesh.
I choose instead to stand on the rock
that sits much higher than I;
in full armor
prepared for battle;
knowing I can do all things through Christ who strengthens me.

I refuse to seek comfort in the traps of the enemy.
I will take refuge in my strong tower,
my fortress;
and look to the hills from whence cometh my help;
a very present help in troubled times.

I open my heart completely,
without hesitation,
yielding
to my loving Shepherd
who leads and guides
offering still waters,
green pastures,
the wings of eagles,
and rest
in the shadow of The Almighty.

For a day in thy courts is better than a thousand. I had rather be a doorkeeper in the house of my God, than to dwell in the tents of wickedness. For the Lord God is a sun and shield: ;the Lord will give grace and glory: no good thing will he withhold from them that walk uprightly. O Lord of hosts, blessed is the man that trusteth in thee.

Psalm 84:10-12 (KJV)

It's Not About Me

℘

My grip on a self-propelled aim
for the world's version of success
has loosened,
given way
to acceptance
of a more divine direction
through a sincere Kingdom connection

My desire is to serve
Be salt
Show light
Share truth
Stand Firm
Know God
Love Agape style
With no plan for retreat

Focus on those
In need
With pain
Holding on to shame
Refusing to claim the name Of the One who gave
His all on the cross

My charge is clear . . . Share the Good News
with all who are near/have ears to hear
And continue in humble pursuit
of the purpose
Specifically laid before I was fearfully and wonderfully made

It's not about me anymore
My Savior has replaced my own image
In my mind's eye
And I've found peace
Beyond anyone's comprehension
And the courage to go on—Find strength in the face of adversity

I've shed the layers of excuses
for selfishness that led me to unyielding sadness
and draped myself instead in true garments of praise

It's not about me anymore
Whewwwww . . . Thank you Lord, I am saved.

Teach me, O LORD, the way of thy statutes; and I shall keep I unto the end. Give me understanding, and I shall keep thy law; yea, I shall observe it with my whole heart. Make me to go in the path of thy commandments; for therein do I delight. Incline my heart unto thy testimonies, and not to covetousness. Turn away mine eyes from beholding vanity; and quicken thou me in thy way.

Psalm 119:33-37 (KJV)

Teach Me

Teach me to number my days, O Lord
To stop
And breathe in the blessings before me;
No longer rely on the time I think I have but don't
Which robs me of pure moments of joy
As my mind races for the future

Embolden me
To say the things I need to say
The moment I need to say them
To whom they need to be said

Take my life
Order my steps
Use me
That I might show the love You have shown me
Without limits
Without conditions

Give me a glimpse of my heart
The instant
It reflects an image other than Yours
That I might immediately yield to the Spirit
Who leads
Those who want to follow

Teach me now, O Lord
That I might one day hear,
"Well done."

I will praise thee; for I am fearfully and wonderfully made: marvelous are thy works; and that my soul knoweth right well.

Psalm 139:14 (KJV)

Who I Am

℘

i am a child
of the Most High God,
an heir of the creator of the universe,
My Abba Father,
who carefully crafted me in my mother's womb
and paved my way to eternity
through His son's sacrifice
long before I ever began fighting my way
into this world.

i know i have purpose—to serve
to bless
to praise His Holy name—the name above every other name

no,
i'm not the person you once knew
unsure
insecure
submersed in the shadows
afraid to live up to the meaning of my name
and shine
for fear of blinding others

my light beams
and i refuse to dim it

i know the order of my steps is divine
because my walk is straight
and i no longer lean
on my own understanding

I am allowing my ways to acknowledge
my Jehovah: provider
healer
redeemer
and my heart reflect my Lord . . . my Savior . . . my friend . . . my Jesus
who shed His blood
that i might find freedom
to run
to dance
to be
a new creation
who's shaken off my former self
and put on the image of Christ

my past is released
i'm not taking claim
of the pain
that i once allowed to define me

i find comfort on my knees
at the foot of the cross
and wisdom when i need it
if and when i humbly ask.
i am the receiver of grace every day
when i truly allow myself to see it.

i know who i am
i am
a child of the Most High God.

For God so loved the world that he gave his only begotten Son, that whosoever believeth in him should not perish, but have everlasting.

John 3:16 (KJV)

CPSIA information can be obtained at www.ICGtesting.com
Printed in the USA
BVOW05s1733200714

359673BV00001B/2/P